Three Symphonies

Tony Conran

(Compiled in 2011)

AGENDA EDITIONS

Published by Agenda Editions
The Wheelwrights, Fletching Street, Mayfield,
East Sussex TN20 6TL
2016

Design and production by JAC design
Crowborough, East Sussex

Printed and bound in Great Britain by
TJ International Ltd, Padstow, Cornwall

Front Cover: painting,
Mynydd Maendy
by Mary Lloyd Jones,
courtesy of Martin Tinney
Gallery, Cardiff

By the same author

Poetry: *Formal Poems* (Christopher Davies 1960), *Poems 1951-67* (Deiniol Press & Gee and Son 1965-7 & 1974), *Spirit Level* (Christopher Davies 1974), *Life Fund* (Gomer 1979), *Blodeuwedd* (Poetry Wales Press 1989), *Castles* (Gomer 1993), *A Gwynedd Symphony* (Gomer 1996), *A Theatre of Flowers* (Gomer 1998), *Eros Proposes a Toast* (Seren 1998), *The Shape of My Country* (Carreg Gwalch 2004), *Red Sap of Love* (Carreg Gwalch 2006), *What Brings You Here So Late* (Carreg Gwalch 2008)

Drama: *Branwen and other Dance Dramas and Plays* (Carreg Gwalch 2003)
The Angry Summer by Idris Davies (Illustrated edition, edited and introduced by Tony Conran, University of Wales Press 1993)

Translations: *The Penguin Book of Welsh Verse* (1967) re-issued and expanded as *Welsh Verse* (Seren 1986 and 1993), *Eighteen Poems of Dante Alighieri* (Tern Press 1975), *The Peacemakers,* selected poems of Waldo Williams (Gomer 1995)

Critical Works: *The Cost of Strangeness* (Gomer 1982), *Frontiers in Anglo Welsh Poetry* (University of Wales Press 1997), *Visions and Praying Mantids* (Gomer 1997).

Biographical Note

Tony Conran (1931-2013) was an ambitious and accomplished poet, a daring Modernist, in the line of Pound, Bunting, MacDiarmid and David Jones. An outstanding translator of Welsh language poetry, *Penguin Book of Welsh Verse* (1967), he built on the radically different relationship between the poet and society he found there to create a distinctive, powerful and humane poetic vision. His many volumes of poetry include *Blodeuwedd* (1988), *Castles* (1993) and *What Brings You Here So Late* (2008). He was also a perceptive and often challenging critic, a dramatist and an influential teacher at the University of Bangor in North Wales.

Born in India, Tony Conran was brought up in Liverpool and Colwyn Bay, and worked for a short time in Chelmsford before settling in Bangor. He was deeply interested in music – classical and folk traditions; science – including botany, chemistry and geology; theology and political theory. He translated Dante and Latin poets as well as Welsh poetry.

Acknowledgements

Thanks are due to the editors of the *Journal of Cloth and Culture* for the publication of 'Fabrics Symphony 8' and to the Red Poets' Society for publication of a selection from 'Everworlds Symphony 9'. Selections from 'Everworlds' have also appeared in *Agenda*.

The Conran Poetry Chorus first performed 'Fabrics' in Bangor and Chester and selections from 'Everworlds' in Bangor and Holyhead under the direction of the author.

Thanks are due to Jeremy Hooker for his excellent introduction, Tony Brown for his support and guidance and Patricia McCarthy for her continuing enthusiasm for Tony's work.

Preface by Tony Conran, 2011

Even as a young man I was already haunted by the idea of a long poem in several disparate movements, like a symphony in music, each movement perhaps similarly subdivided, rhythm against rhythm, style against style, even subject against subject, yet making perfect formal and artistic sense, a balance of viewpoints of essentially one subjective world, yet also a dynamic work of art exhibiting purpose and humanity.

My Symphonies are, more by luck than good management, the classical nine.

Symphony 1	Day Movements: A Choreography for Voices – radio ode (1966-67).
Symphony 2	Castles: Variations on an original theme (1989-90).
Symphony 3	Wager in Heaven: Referendum 1979 (1990-94, revised 2002, 2008).
Symphony 4	Becca (1993, revised 2002, 2008).
Symphony 5	A Gwynedd Symphony (1996).
Symphony 6	What Brings You Here So Late? (as a work in progress known as 'Tarot'), (1997-2004).
Symphony 7	The Magi, (2004).
Symphony 8	Fabrics (in one movement of sonnets), (2006).
Symphony 9	Everworlds (including 'Requiem' for Robert Graves), (2007).

Contents

Jeremy Hooker

Three Symphonies: An Introduction

The scope of Tony Conran's *Three Symphonies* is immense. For this reason, it is essential to begin an introduction with a sample of the combined clarity and mystery that constitute its special beauty. 'Purpose' from 'The Magi' provides an example:

> Is there a reason
> For us?
> Like a hiraeth
> For the one shy kiss
>
> Of first love, the question's
> Beyond our imagining –
> The first What-must-have-been –
> The first lovesong –
>
> The first time I was shown
> The cherry tree
> Of the world
> Bending, flowering insanely
>
> White around us
> Like a brocade of stars,
> My mother's canopy
> And me in her arms …

This is lyrical, but it is not an isolated lyric. As a movement of 'The Magi', and a part of *Three Symphonies* as a whole, it plays a variation on the central theme of the gift of love. Here, love between mother and child, but also love, in a sense close to Dante, as the power that drives the universe. 'White around us' invokes the Muse, the White Goddess, present throughout the symphonies. As a powerful work of the imagination, *Three Symphonies* asks, with longing ('hiraeth'), the question of ultimate meaning, 'Beyond our imagining'.

Three Symphonies completes a work of epic scope, the nine symphonies constituting the centrepiece of Tony Conran's ambitious life work as a poet. The first was *Day Movements,* 1967, and the second *Castles,* 1993. *All Hallows,* 1995, was subsequently revised to form the third and fourth symphonies, *Wager in Heaven* and *Becca*. The fifth and sixth symphonies are *A Gwynedd Symphony,* 1999, and *What Brings You Here So Late?,* 2008. The present book consists of 'The Magi', 'Fabrics' and 'Everworlds', composed in the period 2004–2007. The nine symphonies comprise many movements and are formally and tonally various, rich in subject matter and inventive metaphor. Together they constitute a single, complex vision.

To understand Tony Conran's achievement we must recognize that he cannot be 'placed' with reference to the dominant mode of post-war English verse, which he called 'the anglicising school of self-expression'. His modernism acknowledges diverse influences, including Eliot and Yeats, Robert Graves and the Idris Davies of *Gwalia Deserta* and *The Angry Summer*. But, while finding support in the work of these poets, he used what he found in them creatively in making poetry of striking originality. In Welsh verse, of which he was a major translator, he discovered an attitude to poetic making, and a relationship between poet and society, that were radically different from English models. Readers of this book will encounter a distinctive poetic personality, but it is not that of the first-person lyric, confined to a single individual's experience. *Three Symphonies* draws on their maker's life-story, but as part of the story of life itself, and with an objectivity that subsumes personal emotion in a larger rendering of human experience in relation to the natural and divine creation. What Conran enacts in these poems is a sacred drama.

'The Poem as Symphony', a chapter in his book *Visions & Praying Mantids,* 1997, discusses the models Conran found in instrumental music for the work he desired to write. 'I wanted to write long poems with the weight and shaping authority – what Northrop Frye calls the "encyclopaedic form" – of the traditional epic.' He expresses this succinctly in his unpublished book 'Poetic Forms': 'Mahler's saying that a symphony should contain the world was the key I was looking for'. In *Visions & Praying Mantids* Conran observes that Schubert's *Lieder* and Song Cycles 'demonstrated how a sequence of lyrics could become much greater than the sum of its parts. It could tell a story, uncover psychological drama, make a choreography of moods'. Symphonies consist of 'sequences of independent movements that yet complemented one another to build up a single imaginative unity'. 'Movements' is a key word for understanding the structure of *Three Symphonies*. As in a musical symphony, the work's series of movements is 'dynamic like different acts of a play'.

Epics, in Conran's words, 'deliver us from the scatter of lyric moments, the divorce of the individual sensibility from what is public and social'. Through his study and translations of Welsh poetry he became especially sensitive to epic as a form of poetry written for and about a people, and concerned with their history and destiny. In the case of Wales, epic is integral to their survival as a nation. *Three Symphonies* reflects Welsh experience – indeed, is haunted by it, especially through images and motifs of the Celtic Otherworld; but it is far from being exclusively concerned with Wales. The symphonies' encyclopaedic form includes everything, from the Big Bang to the present parlous state of the world. 'The Magi' in particular is concerned with both cosmic and biological acts of creation, with the whole life-process in time and the sexual production of the human organism. It draws wittily and excitingly upon the languages of biology and geology. A major theme is the contrast and interaction between time and the timeless. The symphonies render poetically the 'benaturing' of God. The marriage of male and female in the Incarnation culminates in 'Everworlds'.

Three Symphonies is a richly imaginative work about the work of the imagination. Its movements both enact and explore creative processes, as we see in the materiality of 'Fabrics', which renders the procuring and preparation of the fleece and other fabrics with which the fashion designer works. Here, too, Conran expresses his sense of the connections that make human society, as in the relation of 'fashion to political, economic and social change'. He is a political poet with a Marxist awareness of material social processes and their cost in human terms. This harmonises with his fundamentally religious sense of human and divine creativity.

A note to 'Fabrics' helps to define the kind of poet Tony Conran is:

> Costume-making/designing is one of the oldest sacred arts, like singing, drumming and dancing – and poetry – as part of a shamanistic ritual. There are pictures in the cave-paintings of men dressed as deer or antelopes, wearing animal masks. As artists, we still perform something of this function, though its sacredness is only vestigially felt. We both create new feeling-patterns for the living to walk in, and reassure the dead that we still belong. They can safely give ground to the new imaginative world that the living need.

The two-way connection between the living and the dead described here – the 'belonging' – affirms the existence of a universal order. This takes us back to what Conran perceived as Welsh civilization, of which 'the central arch' was 'the giving and receiving of gifts, like the giving and receiving of poetry itself'. In accordance with this belief, the celebration of gift and giver is central to *Three Symphonies*. 'The Magi' refers to the gift-bringers, introducing three symphonies that celebrate the gift of life. There is nothing sentimental about this: the gift includes pain and old age and death. But life in time comes with intimations of 'everworld', which the poet glosses as 'the Otherworld life of the imagination'. This is the timeless realm that brings a hauntingly magical quality to *Three Symphonies,* in which, as in Celtic myth, it is manifested through imagery of birds and islands, and flowering trees and whiteness, and associated predominantly with women.

To talk in terms of its big subjects is to risk making *Three Symphonies* sound solemn. This would be to give a totally false impression. Tony Conran is a witty poet, humorous and highly intelligent, with a wonderfully surprising and playful use of metaphor. He has described Idris Davies's form in *The Angry Summer* as 'the symphonic epic mosaic'. 'Mosaic' aptly describes the form of *Three Symphonies* too, as long as it is understood to refer to the dramatic placing of tesserae, not their static fixity. The movements of Conran's mind in the poems are like a dance. The lyrical sections of *Three Symphonies* resemble dance steps. Yeats's poetry of the dance and the dancer is especially important to Conran in this respect, the more so because he shared Yeats's desire to speak to and for his people.

Dance is a ritual, an art of community. Collingwood called it 'the mother of arts', to which Conran adds: 'Every other art derives from dance, or once formed the background to it. Every other art is the better for remembering dance as its inheritance'. Of himself, he has written:

> … being physically spastic has made most of my imagery kinaesthetic – I have been forced to feel in terms of physical movement rather than sight or hearing. I don't dance … But my poetry I've always thought of as a dance for the tongue and the vocal chords: ultimately, since tongue and vocal chords don't occur in a vacuum, for the whole body, the whole mind.

Three Symphonies concludes with a lyric in which a woman addresses God as 'Mr Nijinsky', asking: 'will you dance for us?'. The last words of the book are:

> 'Yes,' said God,
> 'I will dance you your peace.'

Three Symphonies may be described as a dance of the intellect and imagination, with a recurring but varied patterning of images and phrases and motifs. Chief among the latter is the motif of woman. To describe it as image or motif, however, is inadequate, for the presence of the female pervades the symphonies. Tony Conran is a Muse poet, in the sense described elaborately and imaginatively by Robert Graves in *The White Goddess*. Speaking of himself as a young man, Conran said : 'the struggle in my soul was between the Muse and God … the Goddess was everywhere – in the cry of curlews, in the smile of a girl, in the darkness out of which I created poems'. The Second Movement of 'Everworlds', called 'Passage to Dejà', after Robert Graves's home in Mallorca, is in memory of Graves. In 'To the Utmost', a poem in this Movement, Conran writes:

> Hound I was on a vixen earth
> Running to-fro, puzzling
> Through poems –
>
> – and I a callow-hopeful thing –
> But Graves like an elder brother
> Among my doubts
>
> Egged me on
> To the utmost of my reach
> To try
>
> In my own 'living name'
> Poetry …

As these lines testify, it was Robert Graves who confirmed Tony Conran in his vocation as a Muse poet, dedicated to service of the Moon Goddess in all her phases.

Unlike Graves, Conran's Catholicism makes him a highly imaginative poet of the Incarnation. If there could be one lyric that summarises these lucid but mysterious, profound and playful symphonic poems, it would be 'As Dewe in Aprille':

> The Jesu moves down the
> Waters, down the dark
> Channels of Miriam, and
>
> As embryo – as every
> Embryo – re-enacts
> Earth's genesis
>
> When the Holy One
> Nosed through the blackness
> Of unborn stars
>
> Out from the everworld
> Into the cry
> Of a drop of dew.

In his birth, Jesu, son of Miriam (Mary), 're-enacts/Earth's genesis'. True to his vision, Conran links biology and religion in the process of cosmic generation. Expressed in these terms, the creation of the world, 'out from the everworld', was a profoundly imaginative act. We can perceive the mystery in 'a drop of dew'. The poet is not saying we can understand it, for it is 'beyond imagining'. He is not a religious literalist. He is, however, a poet with a sense of the sacred gift of life, which he apprehends and seeks to comprehend imaginatively. This is what Tony Conran does in these wonderful poems, which explore the making of the world and all that it contains.

Symphony 7

The Magi

(The Lindie Sequence)

2004

for Lindie
and the glory of God
benaturing himself
in the world

The Magi

Magi brought gifts
To me, to you,
To the baby, Mab Darogan,
Jesu –

Gold for the King,
Incense
For the Priest, myrrh
For the Victim.

All of us
Magi to one another,
Each one under the star
The Child we journey to.

Prologue

A self she does not know
she has to find

What is home to a moth? A precise,
A chosen plant
Without leaves, maybe, for the chill
Season, gaunt

As a man of bone; yet the moth
Mother lays
For the springtime, on the not yet
Leaf she knows –

Knows, or does not know. Or knows
Just the rich
Ghost of a taste, a slow walk
Down the full stretch

Of her memories, a mouth,
A mumbled twig …
And beyond mouth, the not experience
Of a bare egg.

Dylan Variations

... enter again the round
Zion of the water bead
'A refusal to mourn'

1

And God said –
'Enter, little soul,
Enter the white milk, the wet places,
Soft shit.

Enter a smile, dear swastika
Of elbowing legs,
Go into loud fear
And nakedness.

Enter the wind's juddering.
Go into outside,
Into bloodburn of frost, crumbling
Silk dapple of May.'

God said, 'Through
Time's sliding doors
Enter the room
You have made for me.'

2

And God said –
'Enter again, dear soul,
The backward dark
Before your begetting.

Humanise that mirror in me:
The haploid
Busyness of sex
In gamete land.

Tell its legends
Into your consciousness.
Enter again
The mirroring stories

You borrow for love.
Ancestral voices
Calling in the caverns
Of inwardness –

Do this.
Fly.
Join together.
Or die on the stones.'

3

'Enter again,' says God, 'the whirligig
Of sperm,
The crowding vortex, the busy
Dark of genes…

With the still gaze of love
Beyond that
Stand motionless
In the cloning

Conspiracy
Of amoeba.
Enter again what buds
In your being alive.'

4

God said,
'Humanise
The clone in me –
Bacteria

The first corrupters
That made oxygen
For you to breathe.
And beyond that,'

God said,
'Enter again
The dancing valencies,
Molecules

Tiptoeing into
Existence
Out of ionic flux.
And beyond that.'

5

'Ah,' God sighed,
'Enter again the round
Atom, the ledges
Of uncertainty,

The infinite regress
Of all possible paths,
All destinations. Dear heart,
You ask for a Way.

Humanise in me
The frustration
Of No Way. But the fabric still holds.
Enter again the round

Stage, play out your play
Detached and watchful
Second to second
In your quanta of moment.'

6

'And beyond that,'
God whispered,
'Enter again the round
Zion of light,

The red shift
Of conflagration
That over fifteen million millenia
Is whittled

To a cold noise. Enter again
The round
Zion, the Otherworld
Under the hill.'

The Curlew

How long does it take,
How many thousands of years,
To prepare the eternal moment

On a day when the curlew returns?
                              (after Jeremy Hooker)

Your quadratic equation, Jeremy
– Ignoring infinities –
Has two answers: fifteen billion
Or none at all. Curlews

And days being what they are,
Liminal things,
Shore birds, limiting the ocean's
Shire with thin songs

And the sun's yelping hunt through the void
With fences of dark –
Curlews and days bear witness well
To the primordial work,

The finger of God, with the universe
A drop of his sweat,
A spark of darkness, falling
From the savagery of his light.

The Big Time

That's the small answer: fifteen
Billion years,
With all their price tags,
Afters and befores,

Ago's and soons, last times, next times –
Memberable history
But a future we're not
Co-opted to.

So the big answer is, No time at all –
A function of *i*,
The imaginary number
Which sets you

Right-angled to space-time
Sprouting out
To-fro dimensions, like
A route

Back into the future,
A stroll
Into the lost Now
Of the Holy.

Ah, on that bluff of time
It's breaking dawn;
On the ashen Himàlaya
A lean

Goatherd, ash-white as the rock,
With two hands
Fingers a flute. He
Angles the dance

Of a world his buskined feet
Lift and twist to.
Lord of the meeting rivers,
Shiva,

The fasting god,
Tragedian,
Destroyer of worlds,
Illusionist –

'Come!' I want to say,
On the parapets of home,
'My lord white as jasmine,
Come!'

East

i.m. Tony East

In a Bedfordshire lane, a rabbit of a boy
From a public school
Hopeless and bullied once too often
Was running away.

Fox faces, Jack-by-the-hedge
Leered at him. Buzzard mewings
Of authority
Looked no further than prey.

Young East running, stumbling, gasping
From Marathon
Till his knees cracked under him
And the swish of a car

All but bruised him…
He could run no further.
In the gateway of a wood
Despair flagged him down.

World suddenly sang out.
The thick globe of the melting earth
Was a speck of bright dust,
Then nothing –

Everything – a single leaf
On the God tree
Shimmering – a single wordlessness
Beyond creation.

How long he stared at God
In those seconds
Of ordinariness
He could not say.

But from now on
The only authority
Was gentleness.
He giggled, giving

Credit to the innocent, laughter
To the mistaken.
From all bullyboys,
Jacks in office,

Louts, he walked clear.
He taught little children
To play and read,
And at fifty-five

Went into the light
That will be before the world
And is
Since the beginning.

The Goddess

A time-scale in years:
Fifteen billion, back
To the Creation,
Big Bang, or what you will.

Ten billion after that
To a thin-skinned earth.
And then life,
Say, two billion after that.

And once cells had nuclei
With their Precious's
That like relay runners
They'd to hand on –

Chromosomes, the gene-bearers
Like miniature Hobbits,
Talismans
Against disordering Time –

Then, perhaps one billion
Years ago,
Sex, and the yearning of gametes
To mingle and selve.

Life

It has taken me time

Wherever life grew first –
In black smokers
Of the rifting seabeds
Where bubbling lavas

Geyser up
Into an airless murk;
Or by breakwaters
The soup of lagoons

Warmed by the Sun, but saved
From the deadly light
Under rock debris
Or buried in mud

– Wherever the thin whiskery
Haze of the protein
Replicators
Crept like rottenness

Into sharp stone
Foul-smelling – but
There were no noses –
The secret changelings,

The cloned effluvia
From whose myriads
Came our breathable air,
Our shielded home…

Came, like the locust swarms,
Eventually, us.

Purpose

Is there a reason
For us?
Like a hiraeth
For the one shy kiss

Of first love, the question's
Beyond our imagining –
The first What-must-have-been –
The first lovesong –

The first time I was shown
The cherry tree
Of the world
Bending, flowering insanely

White around us
Like a brocade of stars,
My mother's canopy
And me in her arms.

Legends of Gamete Land

... those other human beings

Gametes are the true
Archetypes:
They have no history
Except hope

In the repetition
Of process.
Time is cyclical,
Space

Is the topography
Of our bodies.
The romance of Gamete
Country

Casts its glamour, its glimmering
Tragedy
Over all
We do.

The Oath

Our gametes crowd us in.
The egg cell journeys
To its throne-room
Down the red passages.

A day and a day
The princess waits.
Promulgates edicts
To distant courts –

How they sing of her,
Virgin queen,
Sithenyn, silk Sally
Down Love Lane!

Her incompleteness
Waits, crumbles
Into ruin. In her equipage
Of blood she must stumble

Soon from her mercy seat,
Die on the steps
And be flotsam, where the waste sea
Of Time laps.

She, for her moment, is One
All alone
And never more
She'll be so.

But if her suitors come,
The gametes
Of a man, alien, homing
Where she waits

Then, perhaps… This hope,
This death,
Is the yoke they put
Like an oath

Sworn for us, the big people,
Two by two,
Driving like oxen
The cutting plough.

The Island

Gametes impose a geography
On women,
On big people. They sculpt
The human

Into landscape, hills, rivers,
Under the air.
Metaphor. Time itself
Is metaphor

For gametes have their own history
Or lack of it.
Their moon cycles
Celebrate

Nothing unique. The same dark,
The same crescent,
The same full. Rotating birth and death
In Russian roulette

As each spin recovers the landscapes
Of the last:
A glade among elms,
A dreamfast

Flowering of the rose.
Then the view,
The climb, the country
Below you

A woman supine, breasts, hills,
Valleys, wide fields
That the circling silver sea
Enfolds.

And last, this island shrunk
To a rock
In the biting thunders
Of earthquake

And tidal wave. The woman
Is half nothing now
As the dragon of time eyes its
Bespoken prey.

But a wrecked ship breaks on the reef.
Screams of the drowning
Like floating raindrops
In the wind's wailing

Carry to shore. No means of counting
Their fate,
No way of knowing what sailorboys
Died in that night.

But perhaps, in the first light of day
One tattered hand
Will clutch – not like flotsam –
Knees stretch and bend

And the Crusoe of the island
Wake to his kingdom.
His footprints chart history.
He's home.

Giant

The man mountain? Or the Cerne
Giant at leisure
Stalking her dry gullies
To pleasure her

With the thunder of his coming?
The gametes chalk him
On her topography. Their
Imaginations walk him

Across the downs. Month by month
They clear the cut
Of his erection with the half-moons
Of their lusty wit.

He's a rain maker.
As he chats up the land
Dry grass perks gratefully. Runnels
Round flints ripple and bend

With the first downpour of wet
As the storms break it
Across her. His penis is Cape
Canaveral, a rocket

Launch, a conquistador.
His eyes prospect
For gold the Mexico of her
Waiting disc.

            But (to misquote)
Does he protect
The land, or is it the land
Protecting him?

Unemployed

Like a thrush, without territory
He can't sing. Queues
Outside auditions –
Job interviews

In the undergrowth, waiting
In case… in case… What?
Maybe an accident –
A joy rider – some lout

Of a sparrowhawk –
Out of nowhere
Right in the shopping mall
Clobbers the Star.

Parody of us, the lead
Male (and the also-ran
As much as the Champ
In Gamete Land)

Is a fact of her geography.
She claws out the chalk
On the hills to image him,
To set him to work

Or to hide his pride
Under the low bushes
To masturbate, and curse,
And spare her blushes.

The Coming of the Big People

Sex is a haploid matter,
Which Big People share
Only at gamete
Convenience.

But social behaviour,
Intelligence,
Consciousness
And love

Are diploid inventions,
Not even prefigured
In the helter-skelter
Of gametes.

Big People aren't just figments
Of the menstrual gyre.
We have history. Detached
From the cycles of fire

In an ancient, diploid
Standing back,
We lend ourselves
To sex,

Not wholly defined by it
As gametes are –
An irony, a longing
Of an ape for a star.

Tongue

I have wanted to respond

I watched my baby
A neonate
Two day's old, focus
On my face, wake

To the dance of my mouth.
I was a suitor
A foot away, calling her
Onto the floor

For the first waltz. I proffered her
A tongue –
Something she had too.
For a long

Moment she studied that tongue.
One day
She would offer her hand, a smile,
A say so

In a vocabulary of gesture
Not dreamt yet.
Now she located her own tongue,
Played it

Her trump of Hearts, tipped it
Towards me once
– Satisfactorily –
And joined the dance.

Hide and seek

Behind this chair – quick –
She cutches down,
She knows the score. Being found
Is both safe haven

And challenge. Found
Is being not lost
For ever and ever
On her pretend island's

Emptying coast –
Her mumless, daddyless sea.
But, being found, after
Squawks and tickles,

She must search next,
Must hide her eyes
In a trance of expectation
– 'No, she's looking –

Till we count ten
You're not to look'…
She's not looking now.
She goes alone

To the unthreaded
Oracular maze –
Her eyes shut, Sybil
Of four years,

Her fingers tight
With the ache of the god
Of Not Looking. Hears them count
Five. Six. Seven. Eight…

Puberty

First time my kitten came in season
All the world knew it.
Shiftless strangers, mean-looking
Paparazzi,

Sidlers on sheds, fence-squatters,
Pimps, whisky priests,
A Soho of mange and voyeurs,
Half-earless piss-artists –

There seemed no end to the
Publicity
Like a royal wedding
Or Princess Diana.

And she, my kitten, inside
When she chose,
On the back of an armchair
Needled her toes

Demure as Fanny Price
While huge Cassius
Our black one-eyed wanderer
Blew kisses

Adoringly from the seat.
He instructed her
For what seemed days,
Tom Troubadour

Of *amour chatois.*
Sex when it came
At backdoor or yard
Public as fame –

Tom after Tom
Took her by the scruff
And trod – trod – trod –
Till with a squawk

And a swipe her anger
Brought brutally
To an end his triumph
And her indignity

While the offended Queen now
Played the whore,
Rolled in the public dirt,
Mewling her pleasure.

*

When my daughter came on,
Even I,
The only male in the house,
Didn't know.

Rumour and corner
Whisperings,
Mother instructions,
A worry, a bravado

Of normality,
A wry flavour ...
I had to be told.
They did me that favour.

But already the door was ajar,
The landscape
Of Gamete country
Taking shape

Just beyond her solitude
A twilight
Between acknowledgement
And secret night.

Period, not full stop,
Comma
In a continuum of eros,
A gap, a caesura

Through which bleedings
Private life
Loomed like a parallel world –
Estrangement, yet venue

For extra-mural footage
– Dear heart, how like you this? –
Love's unpublicity
Opening to a kiss!

The Nuptial Dance

Like the hermit crab, she
Borrows a *this*
From the pebble world
Of *these*

To tuck her tail into,
Her soft vulva
Like a put-away chalice,
A cornucopia.

And is that the *this*
That she is?
No, she grows with the tides'
Proclivities;

She tastes the scuttling shrimp,
The worm, the larva
Of whelk; she nibbles
And stretches further,

Grows too big for that *this*
To shield,
Steps out of it like a skirt,
Bare-arsed and cold

As the long-fingered sea
Puddles her sex –
She dances a *that*
In the world of *those*.

She flutters into air,
She is fledged,
She dances like a grebe,
Sunlit, uncaged

Along the lakes of time.
Two-headed
With her love, she skims
The starry heavens.

She is naked with light.
Nebulae
Crown her hair, the black
Disc shines free

Between her thighs.
Her breasts float,
She is bee. A young
Queen in flight

Leads the drones
In the dance
Of Time's beginning ...
Now and once

She is actual; but their
Potential worlds
In myriads fail,
Fall back, cold

On the stones; and die
In the thin sun
Like a soup of sperm.
All but one –

Her hero. She claims him
For her own,
Reaches for him, and together
Spirals down

To the sensuality
Of earth,
The tenderness
Of the hearth.

Was *that* the dance
That she is?
Her wings are heavy
And proximities

Require her to hive.
In the childering grass
She births, bites off her vanes,
Settles for *this*.

The Gods

Our developing consciousness brooding
On death, on self
And the alien
Salt gulf

Of our beingness –
Banished
From forest to seashore,
Seashore to savannah,

A predator destroying
As he goes,
Peter Pan
Of an ape

Naked, half-hooved,
Half web-toed,
Running on two legs against
All right-minded

Mammal custom,
Throwback
To the dinosaurs,
An unfeathered bird ...

This strangeness
Clicked him
Like a camera lens,
Opening

To unexpected moments
In another
World or existence
Altogether,

A visionary earth,
Dreams,
Hallucinations,
Ghosts –

That numinous room
Where gods
Speak, and the Holy One
Flames from the unburning bush.

Miracle Play

A metaphor transparent to
transcendence

Windows into godhead
Are, in their transparence,
Gods. Angels
Onto clarified air

Impress like wit
Their presence
On us, a stagecraft
Fit for their importance

But in the last resort
Only costume,
Greasepaint, a scripted cry –
'Room, give room!'

How can the triviality
Of an actor, jealous,
Egotistical,
Superstitious

– Like the rest of us –
Give us Cordelia
In his arms, the crumpled
Peripeteia –

Prithee, undo this button?
How can that vanity
Die into this?
We look into

The eyes of a god to ask it –
The painted eyes
Of an angel, sculpting itself
Onto freshening breeze.

Commentary

Of all the old gods, trees
Keep their mirroring
Most, waylay us
In our travelling eyes.

To watch them
Would be a life's work,
A yoga of stretching sight,
The intricacy unique

To that moment, yet
A web of vision
Like always. Their community
Takes us in,

Spellbinds with the whispering
Silence
Of a storytelling too fine
For happenstance,

For history … The day before Whit
My poem. Whitsun fare
For the apostles
Flaming with the unburning fire.

The way through the trees
Concentrated
To a young angel, a sapling ash.
I was drunk
With light, dazzled
With too much darkness

I attend to the tree,
I sway with its stems …

But then later, writing
The poem,
Transfiguration stalled
Like a memory of dreaming,

A lost signifier
To an undeciphered tongue.
I only know
The young branches

Of the ash
Inextricably
Became a oneness of
Your being and the tree.

Visions do not wipe
Realities
But for their moment co-exist
With them.

Welsh paths, stone walls, dead grass
Still fill the frame
Where Gabriel kneels
In a Nazareth yard.

The tree speaks with tongues.
If I tried
To decipher it, the translation
Would be me,
Not your branches, not your being
In a tree.

Mary

We can be in the Jesu,
In Christ;
He is more than a brother,
We are more than his friends.

He tells us he is the vine,
We are the branches
He is the head,
We are the arms and legs.

He rubs our noses
In this
Scandalous mixing of himself
With us.

We have to eat him,
Drink him,
Walk along him like a road,
Die on his cross,

Like Mary, welcoming the Jesu
Against all
Likelihood
Or propriety,

A holy parasite
Into ourselves…

Yet in Mary's priority
Permitting it,
Rounding out
With the physical body of God,

There's a human
Beingness,
A humanity
That's hers alone.

She – merely human
Like us,
One of the Big People –
The hinge of the Door.

The Second Eve

Our first poet, the young
Godbearer, girl
Whose bright eyes were a danger
To the world,

So fine with delight, so
God-lucent, with the force
Of Caruso's top C
They could break glass!

Eve, she who could talk
With snakes, who could name,
Who in nakedness
Trod the round rhymes

Of the Eden-dance,
Who made love
To the first man
In the crab-apple groves –

Eve… but the spears
Of the Cherubim
Turn aside now.
She is at home

In the dust and stone
Of Nazareth,
Oasis, wellspring
On Jewry's path –

Miriam, a teenager
In love with love,
Waits by the apple tree
And the cross-stave.

Ave

*An act of joyful participation in
the sorrows of the world*

The angel had not remembered
Till now,
Facing Miriam like this,
The originality

Of Eden, the physical animal
God was in love with.
This creature for a second
Like a stammer

Queried his status
As messenger,
Avatar or window. A wry
Taste of Satan

Wrinkled the glass:
'You shall be as gods'
– The deft temptation to pride
Of what is true.

Simply an unexpectedness
In the mirror,
That was all. Now he was
Love's emissary

To the world. His mind
Swooped through fifteen
Billion years, down to
The girl beside him.

She had noticed him.
His painted eyes
Met hers.
'Mary,' he said.

The Beast

Often darkness has usurped me and I
have feared a beast in my depths…

Tales were told
Of the conception of great heroes,
Cú Chulainn, Krishna,
Hercules,

By a god,
A shadow trickster,
Eternity's adulterer
In the marriage sheets of time…

Was it Gabriel the go-between
That tirled at the pin?
An' wha sae ready as Mair hersel'
To let Yr Iesu in?

The Father

The Prodigal of worlds,
The holy One,
Did not simply
Lift her into himself –

He does *that*
With the rest of us!
He first in her womb
Concentrated

To play,
In the dances and legends
Of Gamete land,
A strange, incestuous
Love-making, God's
Dealing with his child.

La Figlia Del Suo Figlio

Yet the marvellous child of Incarnation
Dances the spring lanes, singing
Of her love. She bends to a violet.
The eternal whispers her nostril.
Her hand touches a wild rose.
The god bleeds in her fingers.

Now, with the embryo
Of God planted
In the dark tilth
Like a rice root dibbled

Into a paddy –
The angel up to his knees
In time, in the clarty mud
With the concentration of a thief.

The Jesu

Mab Darogan,
Riding on a donkey,
Comes with all the ragtag
And bob-tail

Of a holy people –
Beggars,
Junkies,
Thieves, prostitutes –

From the alley-ways and ditches
To give us, for our birthday
A party
At the cross.

Inching his way through Incarnation,
Benaturing
Himself
In the world

God drives the hills to Ascension,
The benatured Son
Giving the present of his world
To the Father.

The Studio

The sense of sin is a void
In the probity
Of ourselves, not just guilt
What we do

Or do not, and not just shame
Being wrong.
Sin is the talisman
We bring,

The potential of recognition,
The broken
Shilling that matches God's half
Of the token.

We are the sketch that the painter
Laid aside, lost
– Seemingly – dumped in a pile
Of studio waste,

Unfinished daubs that even the Eternal
Would not sign …
But one clear-out, we are pulled
Into the light again

To the clean creativity
Of his glance.
The god remembers
The distance

He put into us, the aching
Possibility
Of transfiguration. We wake
In Gethsemane,

In the garden. The secret police
Have come
With the informer's kiss. One second
Before they name

Us: 'You are Jesus of Nazareth?'
The god hoists us back
To his easel. The tip of his brush
Touches the quick

Of vision within us, and our lips
Have authority to speak.
'Yes,' we hear them say, 'I am he
Whom you seek.'

Via Negativa

He works at death.
Not easy –
God to be dead in this
His creature.

To know nothing –
Not to number
The fungus tattling
To its feast.

Not to delight
In the starry
Bacteria
Crowding

To the horizonless
Singularity
Of his brain, the black hole
Of love.

Down the *via negativa's*
Infinite closure
That Saturday
God stumbled:

Recessional
Of fifteen billion years
To a night where no times
Ticked.

No, not easy.

Death is a creature of time
And here it was,
Crushed into a singularity
Time is not.

Was Death
That Saturday
Suborned
To the horizonless moment?

The edged light
Of the tomb
Opens…

He waits for the first guest.

Symphony 8

Fabrics

in one movement
of sonnets

2006

… We are such stuffe
As dreames are made on –

The Tempest

for Vivien
fashion designer

1

Fleece

You've finally a fleece, emptied it
Like a Peter Pan's grey shadow, across
The stone outhouse floor, stink of shit,
Lanolin, twigs and shrivelling moss ...

And where you'd only scavenged fold
Before, or blackthorn, crawled the run
For wool, prospected like fool's gold,
Or gleaned thin wisps under the sun –

Now, the white mass of it is daunting.
Deciding what to do with wool
Quite suddenly's not meaningful

Except in terms of *you* – your life
On offer from the shearer's knife
Chosen to dye, a cloak you're flaunting!

2

Washing the Fleece

Giant chrysalids, ghosts of future dreams
Hanging like bats, limbering to exist
Into our human world ... Dunked in the streams
Of a zinc tub, surfacing through the mist

Like surf-riders, to a cleanliness
That makes the fleeces biddable to comb
Or card, sprouting like mustard-and-cress –
But so the lanolin's not leached with foam

Until, for want of oil, the spin can't hold.
For spinning's the crux of it, the yarn told,
The life meted out. Chrysalids wait.

Dream, that butterfly, will meet the wheel soon,
And what the spindle like a whirling moon
Decrees of neap and floodtide, take as fate.

3

Dye Plants

Whose accident dropped wool in nettle broth
So it dried yellow? Or had half hours
To hunter-gatherer like a flitting moth
Juices of leaf or berry, tree-bark or flowers

Simmered to a flux? Whose was the vat
Her ne'er-do-well family got a fortune from –
Coloured stuffs, traded at palace or peasant's hut,
Caravanserai to China, to Khartoum?

You go out, searching. Kneel in old spoil heaps,
Wade the rank weeds of a drain, or tenderly
Lift the lichen from wet woods. Set a fire

Like a witch's barbecue in the night. Crouch. Creep
Through a stink of boiling poisons, till you see
With neolithic eyes, your sight's desire.

4

Nakedness is the raw
Material we work at –
Unthread the worm for
And the fleece comb flat.

We write on our nudity
With yarn and dye
The adventuring me,
The tale of my I.

Loved as we hope we are
In the familiar huddle
Of a tribe, yet still

Unassuaged by a cuddle –
A quirk or avatar
Of Aloneness craving its will.

Stone Age

The earliest drape was lyric as a necklace,
Like a flower's bee path, said to the eye,
'Come, honey's here – this way, this way!' A reckless
Swirl of tassels, just shadowing the thigh
Or not, as ripples in a trout stream uncover
As much as hide, the dark hair, the delectable
Halls of the cunt. Flying a kite for a lover,
A mobile at belly-level, episcopal
Robe for a high priestess of sex …

Knotted with string
Like macramé dreadlocks, extending the range
Of short-and-curlies to offer intimacy
At a distance, and bring
Into the workaday of nudity
A choosing openness, laughter-loving and strange.

6

Fashion

Fashion, like all oracles, was ambiguous.
Give or withhold, which was it, bless or hurt?
Teddy-boy, Flower Power, Mod or mini-skirt –
Those auguries that, blind, tormented us

Like news of shifting worlds. Apocalypse
Was surely not on offer, *Götterdämmerung*
No dressage could deliver? And yet, something
Broke in Vietnam, certainties did collapse,

We even got rid of Thatcher. A girl's thighs
Bare to the slender rump and walking proud;
Leatherback Rockers revving in Sussex lanes –

Were they cause or symptom? All the lies
Gathering, the old empires feeding the crowd
Booze or blarney, until Fashion change?

The Oldest Profession

We've no rights, Vivien. Squatters on the outskirts
Of other men's hopes, we've no claim
On the City, no insurance against the hurts
Nothingness or hunger inflicts. Fame or shame
Are only significant in the ability
They give us, or not, to go on – unloose
The next novel, sculpt a stone symphony,
Perform to perfection a frock. Catch in a noose
Of dreams our heart's everyday. Dance the human
On the opening night of the world. Dare to be
In their suchness of moments, a man, a woman …

Let linens go, grieving silks float free
So that we nakedly wait – 'Come buy, come buy –
Beauties for sale!' plead to the passers-by.

8

To us, which was bespoke –
Field of the Cloth of Gold
Or field full of folk?

King Cotton, out of his bole's
Captivity freed
By a Yankee jinn,
Revolutionises greed;
Like Robespierre or Lenin

Promulgates equality –
Blacks as plantation stock,
Whites slaving at mill,
Pay for the democracy
Of a new frock –
Off the peg, bright, dressed to kill.

9

India

She'd worn the memsahib world so carefully –
Club, cards, golf, tennis: sex predation like slugs
In a bed of husbands: the intricacy
Of protocol: tolerance like a drug's …

Yet, when she mentioned India, it was not
The squeaky-white top frippery of the Raj,
But the vast circumambience of what
Went on in brown humanity at large

Tickled affection. Look, this bedspread's left!
The warping, once, straddled a village street
And in a glaze of light – a dusty walkway

For Brahmani bulls humped like toast-racks – all day
Odd villagers with an hour to spare would meet
To shed the warp, let fly the scuttling weft.

10

Dulas Ward

Nurses, colour-coded like parrots or tits,
Squawk through the ward where a deaf man
Zany for attention, cries. Edward sits
Watching a foot flaming with medication
Too painful to sneak out, driven mad
By the jabber of denied tobacco. Bad blood
Or dammed, the heart's service corrupted,
Clotted like roads with cliff-falls of mud –

Our specialities. Losing a leg here,
A life there, we carry our drug pumps
Like purses dangling at the wrist;
Experiment with exo-skeletons,
Articulated Zimmers, push like dung-beetles
To a mobility of lurch and twist.

11

Out of the Holocaust

A priesthood is always ambiguous in time:
It re-inhabits catacombs, re-members
Hurried assemblies round a scribbled shrine.
Pentecost blazed, they say, in these embers –
Third-century Roman mufti, a poncho to go
To the shops in, once dis-identified us, now
A sacred rubric, a silk chasuble like snow
Sewn with a martyr's blood. Past terror is how

We validate our mission. But to put on
Priesthood like this, we must dispense with time.
To God, past or present is nothing. We climb
Traditional paths, invoke half-understood lexicon
To summon him. But it's for a new-born
Swaddling that the chasuble gets worn.

12

We are both priests, Vivien,
Shaman-born. Our crafted
Touch on the nerves – fright
Or courage, enchantment

Or phobia – in trance
To holy places
Guided the dance.
Spirit faces

Crowded us round.
'Look,' we said,
'Our insignia is yours.'

And on futurity's floor
The shuffling dead
Slowly give ground.

13

Retting the Flax

Linen, of all cloth, speaks the tongue of the dead.
Like Ra at sunset, flax limps in the drought.
Flowers that answered the sky with their blue, have set
Seed and withered, brown fingers pull out

The yellowing plants, and women bundle the stems
Onto an ass. Osiris is dead. He must drown,
Must sail in a sunk stone ship, wet realms
Of loss, decomposition, rot down

Days, weeks, till the fibres alone are firm
And visible proto-linen from death
Comes resurrected to the clattering loom.

Cool and uncluttered, linen stays its term
Not easily stained, bleached words in a tomb
– Hush, he's risen. A shroud. Mummy-cloth.

Penelope

A weave of tapestry hangs on the loom,
Each weighted warp growing significance
In the bunched wefts, picturing Troy's doom,
Dead heroes, intricate gods of chance –

The cloth to be memorial, epic stuff
Every day worked on. But every eve
As the shuttle inched to vision, not enough
Glory ached in the threads. How could she leave

An incompleteness, knowing what was lost?
Every night then, creeping from her widow's bed
To the silent loom, she'd unravel the weave –

Odysseus was not in it. Glory or cost
Of glory … But Odysseus was dead,
They told her. Why would tapestry not grieve?

15

Protocol

Initiation is the business of art.
Young girls frighted, each to her solitude
Clutches from word or image what has heart.
A trumpeter's angst makes sense of a world mood.

Yes, but where? From Eleusis dance the dark roads
From rock festival, from gap-year Mexico –
Dance, into home! The agon of the gods,
Bacchus or Hendrix – the small deaths also

You encounter minute by minute – now are calm.
For an instant beyond design or care
You embody what shall be. Words you'll use,

Styles you'll judge wearable. You realise home's
Where the dead feel easy, you the ambassador
For them to the humanity you choose.

16

We are chrysalids
Of our past, unwound
And bobbined from eyelids
And the fingering sound

Of our dreams. Birth
Is what world asks –
That, or our own rebirth
Who cradle dead husks

In the swaddling bands
Of a worm. Crowd on crowd
We go, round and round

Our mulberry galaxy. Hands
Weave and unweave, shroud
With white seed tomorrow's ground.

Symphony 9

Everworlds

2009

The mind, that ocean where each kind
Doth straight its own resemblance find,
Yet it creates, transcending these,
Far other worlds, and other seas ...

Andrew Marvell, 'The Garden'

For Gwilym Morus
and the sweetness of the Spirit,
Harrower of
Imagination and Time

Everworlds

Beyond this Divide

Songs of the Cherubim
Call us, green islands
Beckon us, but once heart
Hears, it's as if
We've been orphaned, lost

To that grey rock and
Lucid wave, shadowy with
Saffron fish,

Where great turtles clamber
Down beaches and are
Sure of tomorrow.

Three Kings

Three kings came round the rocks
Where island birds
Stalk fragile in the foam.

Palaces all left,
They smell warm rotting hay,
A clammy stink of goats,
A tired girl.

And after this, will Time
Subdue them, heads
Bowed down?

Or will they cry lifelong
Like curlews? Carry no gift
In the night

Save the desire for rock,
For dusk-grey stone, and white
Flamingos in the foam?

The Wind

On the blank mind, a blown
Thought scribbles – a girl's
Grace on the blank wall –

Graffiti, or trick of twig's
Shadow? Long everworld
Hair swirls for a moment,

She glances back at me.
Vanishes. A dark shipwreck
Calls me through the storm.

The Poison Glade

Why am I, again and again,
A pilgrim here? Is it
That a branch might blossom

Or suddenly snow be heaped
The length of every twig
And every tread creak white?

Or is it that visions might spark
Up this cold chimney of dreams

Transfiguring waste like a bonfire
Jerked into startled flame?

Migrants

Sometimes I see myself
An infinite regress
Of lovers, stumbling

Like a migration
Of refugees
From plague or famine,

Or the wildebeest
In the dry season,
River after river

Slithering in log-jams,
Mud, and the choosing
Crocodiles.

I hear myself
Like a posse of waders
Plain on the shore.

Wing after wing
Otherselves of I
Beat

Faster or fainter, and
Watch me

A concourse for ever
To this glade in a
Poisoned world.

Lifeline

We should know by now
The heartlessness
Of situations –

Lively love
Buried, ambition
Drugged away easily

Where the conduits
Of nightmare
Drain the sun.

Myselves, at this
Grove of phantoms,
A lifeline of steely

Incantation
Sways. The wind
Huffs and whines

And a dead leaf
Twists its twig
Like a weathercock.

To Walk in Everworld

These Everland waste places
Cannot imagine Time –
For them,

Even to walk, one foot
Like a Pharaoh's
In front of another

Mirrors a cosmos
Of walking, legs'
Infinite regress

Each of them my leg
– My best foot forward –
Aurora borealis

Splashing the sky
With leg, an infinity
Of stepping alone

Into the dark –
No event, no time,
No moment's horizon.

Moonlight

Through the mist, as if
Cleared aside
For a pageant,

A wraith of moonlight
Walks the waves.

From the glass cabinet
Of my tenderness
I look out

On a rolling greyness,
A visible,
Bounded, touchable

Moon of woman …
As if
Outside the clarity

Of glass, knowable
Femininity
Waited

For a new sixth day, a courage, a fresh
Co-existent
Of terror.

The Unicorn

I am climbing a meadow.
St John's wort, hawksbit,
Yarrow and convolvulus

Give way before my feet.
A harebell nods,
Recognises me

As if my step
Sounded in the language
Of its stalk, my name.

I have been here before,
In this Tyrol, dreaming
A déjà vu of centuries.

Dusk is already
Emulsifying
My middle distance

As pieces of sky
Cognate with the world.
Vaguely thunder rumbles.

In my up-ended field
I notice I am not alone.
A white colt – a grey,

Don't they call it? – and
In this tinctured gloom
A grey phantom, a lawn

Wanderer, almost the colour
Of cloud – approaches.
He hangs his head, seeming

Not to look, assessing
My provenance for titbits.
He sways side to side

Uncertain. Friendly enough
So I speak to him, offer
Pax in a handful of grass.

He nuzzles my shoulder.
His eyes are sad,
Mirroring the world

Like a language, a language
No one speaks or replies to,
But not dead, no,

A lingua franca of sorrows,
Two full moons, two tears
Of the Pietà. Then

I notice, behind his eyes,
Or above them perhaps
(It is too faint in the dusk

To be sure) a silver blade,
A dirk – and it seems like vision –
Not my vision, but the grey colt

Seeing his own whiteness
In itself and in a colourless
World, the living moon of grief.

I reach out for the knife
As if it was a horn of plenty
On his forehead, as if

He was offering it me
To drink. Everworld death
Swings in his tossing head.

My hand is bleeding. As I sink
Through the tides of coma
I hear hooves galloping,

Galloping still, leaving
Me drown.

Passage to Dejà

i.m. Robert Graves (1895-1985)

Dejà Unvisited

The hill haunted me. Dejà –
One of my everworlds
Whose magical fauna

Sometimes as friends of friends would come
Filling my room
With his last, dumb

Awarenesses, geologically
Slow, a poetry
Speechless as lichen.

My household could have been translated
And I'd only to look out
Through olive groves

To see twilight
Blur the long stairs
Up to the town,

The corner to his home …
And behind me, did I half-hear
Her footsteps

Who 'variously haunts'
This hill,
This island Earth?

The Erosion of Everworlds

Like evolving life itself
Everworlds erode
To the deep time bottom,

Drop like plankton
Then, atomised, re-enter
By crater and quake

Out, under the moon.
We breathe in, breathe out…
A process like sleep,

A renewal, moment
To moment, of the
Body of dreams…

But that body itself, that wheel
Of radiating visions
We ride on, moves

On its own rocky road
Extinction to
Extinction.

Cultures
Suddenly degrade
(Unbelievable as ice)

To Eschatologies –
The Last Things,
The enemies of ever.

Castle

Beyond the morfa,
Listening to the dreams
Of an everworld ocean

Rhiannon's birds sang
To the mooching I
– Not louder near, not softer afar –

A lang-syne of mother love
Unconscripted by ulterior
Hope or purpose...

But on Harlech hill –
Shops, cottages, slated chapels
Curling round it – end-games

Towered on curtain walls
And, high in the twinned
Gatehouse, played.

Soldier

Fought – to what was
(Near as damn it) death,
Reported dead

Screaming from his wounds,
Hurts that bled
All his life to nightmare

And cut him, sixty years
Later, into a separate world, from
Speech itself, and motion –

In the slow draggle
Towards death, the Warrior's
Timeless battle.

Oxford, 1919

'And in Academia, I too'… Taking
What he wanted, trying on
Broad and High, buskin
And chatterer's sock:

Wading runnels of nightmare, Isis and Somme
Under the willow islets:
Tall swan and coot,
Amorphous haze

Of meadow-sweet and white breath,
Where adventurous bullocks
Suddenly frighted, avalanched
In the broken mud.

For a whole ten seconds, the river's
Heavy red, a freight of corpses
Popping like balloons,
Flowed.

Disembarking

Waiting for the liner to dock
And the Lowry-like matchsticks
To be jerked into motion

As if they were people,
Automatons with luggage
And the faint compulsion

On the bare quayside everworld
To embrace, to pick one's path
Between strangers, to greet

What had come to be greeted,
Unreal as a kiss
In the disabling wind.

From the Calendar of the Tree Alphabet

Beth, birch-month, Dec. 24 to Jan. 20
Luis, rowan-month, Jan. 21 to Feb. 17
Nion, ash-month, Feb. 18 to March 17 …
Onn, gorse-day, spring equinox, a Goddess festival,
a day of initiation

The Goddess Sings

at the Spring equinox

I grew in a primary land of birch
When the day was slender,
And never the hard ground yielded to search
Hint of green splendour.
Only the gaunt and virgin rind
And cruel twig
Betrayed my innermost mind
When the night was big.

Waters carried me through a land of ash
Under Gorse Mountain
To a well where my lips were rash
At witchcraft's fountain:
I am the day and the equal night
And sign of a kiss,
Where the ousel shouts into light
My ninefold bliss.

To the Utmost

Hound I was on a vixen earth
Running to-fro, puzzling
Through poems –

– And I a callow-hopeful thing –
But Graves like an elder brother
Among my doubts

Egged me on
To the utmost of my reach
To try

In my own 'living name'
Poetry
– And I like a jugful of clattering words –

Opening my eyes
Slowly
To the silence.

The Peony

After he died, and the everworlds
Sucked him out like a pipette –
– Every drop of him

From the superficies of time –
On the long rustling journey
To the doubtful isles

Where the warm rock, white egrets in the foam
And vermilion rowan-berries
Gleam like lips of a kiss...

Some years after his death,
Visiting friends, and friends
Of friends in Dejà,

We had tea at his home. The sense
Of his dead presence
Left me tongue-tied.

I gawped round the shrunk Parnassus,
Moved more by a red peony
Than by his books.

He'd found it endemic in the hills,
And for some quirk, personal
Or bardic, magical or

Just because he loved it, bedded it down
In his half-shadowed quiet
Of a lawn:

I could feel his fingers arbitrary
As poet or Celt
As he planted it –

A rubric that might come in handy,
Self-dedication
Or passing fancy –

Who knows? But that effulgence,
That modesty
Of crimson and dark green,

Was the nearest I ever came
To him in person
By the tulip-tree under his eaves.

The Empire of Pain

The Ferret

The Empire of Pain
Sends out emissaries, spies,
Affable merchants.

You spend an hour or so
Wondering
How to be rid of

A button-holing stranger
With a hare-lip
Who refers in a bar

To a life you don't
Remember
Not leading.

The Gospel Makers

The four of us –
  Anna Akhmatova

Annunciation

Angel of train journeys –

Over the dark Steppe
Pasternak, scattering
Windowfuls of light.

Flight into Egypt

Exile
Like a tired child
She dragged behind her

– Marina Tsvetayeva –

Integrity
Awkward like a guy
On a bonfire gesturing

Where the white-smiled
Committee-men

Regulate and lie.

Gethsemane

As if the torturers
Squeezed pain
Like a lemon
On him –

– Osip Mandelstam –

   Scouring out
   Consonants,
Hobbling vowels
With broken thumbs.

Were you there?

And Akhmatova herself, her menfolk
Traipsing their inches between infinities
In a prison yard, when a dazed stranger spoke
Not knowing her, 'Can you describe this?'

Can anyone, this? But to be articulate
Was all she'd left, artist and woman. Can
Anyone, this? Lamentation's mistress, how fate
Waited, coiled like a spring, your 'yes I can.'

The Home

And if you don't know
That it's pain? –

The very old –

Fly-bitten

Like cow pats
By the muddy gate
Of a field –
An everworldless

Day-room
Where dinners come trayed
Like swinging udders

And nurses sit
Milkmaids
On five legs

Talking in two languages –
One, in code
Across corridors,

The other like music, humming
A lullaby of spoons
And Open Wide.

To the Child Jesu

I thought this world was but a toy –
                              Twelfth Night

Holy One –
Moonlight's boy. A star
Danced, you were born.

Your Magi
Lear in the storm. Leech
Gatherer's distance.
Winterreise.

Krishna on the field of war,
And by the wine-dark rockpools
Spartans

Comb their hair.

Mary and John from Golgotha

I was wedged in a place of
loss and mourning, a keening
for what has been or cannot be.

She walked through the night,
Her numb feet
Wedged in the tramline of custom –
Precisely – the street.

A wounded Orpheus in front of her,
A new son
Just broken like dry bread
And put into her hands.

Fourth Movement

Benedictus

As Dewe in Aprille

The Jesu moves down the
Waters, down the dark
Channels of Miriam, and

As embryo – as every
Embryo – re-enacts
Earth's genesis

When the Holy One
Nosed through the blackness
Of unborn stars

Out from the everworlds
Into the cry
Of a drop of dew.

Conscript

How did these everworlds of sorrow
Ever start? Tides lapping
At the edges

Of our imagining, a salt
Bitterness that never forgets
Or arrives at now?

Through the blitzed streets
Of slums
A private soldier

In battle-dress, but on leave
Whistles tunelessly
In the dawn.

Grey boots echo-sound
Round rubble – this neighbour
Or that's known hearth

Like black flotsam, wood
Singed by the sea.
The soldier pays

No heed. Boots
Chart a course
Through the shoals

Of would-be time, yesterdays
Dirtied by loss.
He is walking home.

His eye reaches for it –
Bitterness that never forgets
Or arrives at now.

The Fossil Collector

Like a Bedouin child, God
Walks in the desert.
A blue-faced Tuareg, a gypsy

Of the dust, he makes for
Where he last found humanity,
Oasis, camping ground

In the sub-zero dune.
Through the foam of the constellations
His lantern steers, into every

Deserted tent
The sharp cry of its light
Prizing out love.

Radio Hams

Who was it said, 'Poets
Don't hunger to be admired
But believed'?

So do everworld creatures hunger for time,
Even commit murder
To experience a moment, to

Gulp it down, one jab
Of reality, looking out
From frightened eyes

At the Ordinariness – to them
A splendour
Beyond their imagining.

All the technology of dreams
Devotes itself to this:
Inverting their longing

And tainting our souls with it
So that the poison
Enters us like hunger.

The Everworlds crowd round us
Listening as we transmit
Their music back to them:

Hearing the slight distortion,
Wow or pre-echo
Of our dying,

They scrape it off, and chew it
For the faint taste it carries
Of wasted Time.

God in the Everworlds

God came into the Everworlds.
Nobody noticed him.
'Right,' said God,

And he sat down in the green
Room of a wood
To invent himself –

An impressario of the holy
Dancing like the ripple of leaves
His catkins of folly.

The music of miracles
Flowered like yuccas
White spires of lost causes

Bodying to the dawn
His exuberant disasters
Through a narrative of thrushes.

Revelators of his grace
Hoarse as an oracle
Of crouching toads –

The Master of Ceremonies
Flicking comets
Out of his hat …

God standing in the crater of himself
Like a black meteorite
Of denial.

Everworlders were confused.
They'd crept in to see the show,
And here he was

Facing them out, and yet
Not seeing them, the antique
Unconsciousness of a god.

He held them there. At last
One of them clambered
To the mountain of his silence,

Tugged at his sleeve.
'Mr Nijinsky,' she said,
'Will you dance for us?'

God looked at her. 'Dance?' he said,
'What shall I dance?'
She shrank from him.

Ancient greed in her
Glittered like a sea-creature
Brought up in a net.

'Maestro,' she whispered,
'Will you dance Time for us?
Will you dance Time?'

'Time's a long way off,' said God.
'We dream of it,' she said.
'Some of us have seen it.'

God turned from her, a mountain again
In the distance, a grey
Planet. 'Will you dance for us?'

The mountain breathed softly.
'Yes,' said God,
'I will dance you your peace.'

Notes by Tony Conran

Symphony 7: The Magi:

I have tried to make these notes as accurate as I can, but my primary aim was to write poetry, not science or theology.

p.17 *Mab Darogan* – (Welsh) the Prophesied One (lit. Son)

p.20, 30 etc *Gamete(s)* – Haploid cells or nuclei specialised for fertilization, like our sperm or egg-cells

p.22 *Bacteria ... that made oxygen* – the earth's primordial atmosphere did not contain free oxygen, and therefore the earth was not protected by its allotrope ozone against deadly solar radiation. Oxygen was formed as a by-product of primitive anaerobic life, such as bacteria, until the atmosphere contained enough for more developed creatures to breathe and for the ozone layer to shield them.

p.23 *Ledges of uncertainty* – the orbits or 'shells' in which electrons revolve round an atomic nucleus. In that quantum world, the Uncertainty Principle means that if we know the position of a particle we cannot in principle know its velocity (where it is going and how fast); and if we know its velocity we cannot know where it is. Nevertheless 'the fabric still holds' because, with the huge numbers of particles involved, we can make statistical predictions about the behaviour of matter at any larger-than-atomic level.

p.24 *A cold noise* – radiation from the Big Bang, which, due to the expansion of the universe over fifteen billion years, is now only detectable as very long-wave ('cold') radio 'noise' coming from all directions in space.

p.25 *Quadratic equation* – an equation which involves a square (but no higher power) of an unknown quantity – e.g.

$$x^2 - 4 = 0$$

Typically there are two solutions: in this case, $x = 2$ or -2. It sometimes happens that an equation has infinity as one solution, while its other solutions are finite. In applied maths it is usual to disregard infinite solutions as not relevant. My metaphor is playful and not to be taken too literally.

p.26 *Fifteen billion years* – roughly the age of the Universe. I gather that since I wrote this sequence cosmologists have re-estimated it as 13.7 billion; but poetically I have not thought it worth altering in the text.

p.26 *Shiva* – the third member of the Hindu trinity, Brahma the creator, Vishnu the preserver and Shiva the destroyer. Shiva's sacramental symbol is the lingam, or erected phallus; but he is also the great ascetic and the master of illusion. The titles 'Lord of the meeting rivers' and 'My lord white as jasmine' are like signature tunes in the poems of two South Indian Bhakti saints, Basavanna and the marvellous woman-poet Mahadeviyakka respectively. *See Speaking of Siva*, trans. by A.K. Ramanujan (Penguin Classics, 1973).

p.9, 32 – *Hiraeth* Welsh, virtually untranslatable but usually taken to mean 'longing' but

114

encompasses 'nostalgia' and 'grief'.

p.20, 39 *Haploid* – A description of a nucleus or cell (or by extension an organism) in which chromosomes are represented singly and unpaired. The haploid chromosome number (n) is therefore half the diploid number (2n). See *Gametes*.

p.39 *Diploid* – A description of nuclei or cells (or by extension, organisms, tissues or stages in a life cycle) in which the chromosomes occur as homologous pairs, so that twice the haploid number is present. (In sexual reproduction, diploid cells produce haploid gametes by a process called meiosis, which then pair with others to form a new diploid generation.)

p.40 *Neonate* – a new-born baby, up to three months old

p.51 *Our first poet* – Mary's poem or psalm, the *Magnificat*, which she recited to her older (but also pregnant) cousin Elizabeth, is the first Christian lyric – and indeed, along with those of Zacharias and Simeon which follow it in Luke, practically the only poetry in the New Testament, unless we count the Beatitudes.

p.51 *Miriam* – the Virgin's Hebrew name, translated in the New Testament as Mary

p.53 *Mair* – Welsh for Mary

p.53 *Yr Iesu* – lit. 'The Jesus', the usual name for Christ in the Welsh Bible

p.55 *Figlia del suo figlio* – (It.) daughter of her own son, referring to Mary as both God's child, as we all are, and his Mother because she bore Christ, man and God, as her son

Symphony 8: Fabrics

p.67 *Sonnet 5*. The early stone-age statuettes of women sometimes show these string aprons. Hera borrows one off Aphrodite to seduce Zeus back to her bed in Homer, and the same sort of apron-cum-girdle with hanging tassels is often worn over a flared skirt in traditional peasant dress in the Balkans. My information comes from a marvellous book called *Women's work: the first 20,000 years: women, cloth, and society in early times*, by Elizabeth Wayland Barber (W.W. Norton, New York 1994) in which she says that she was lent one once, and the feeling of sexual power it gave her was quite startling. Perhaps Aphrodite did know her own business best! Of course, the stone-age female statuettes were naked apart from the swirl of tassels hanging round their hips. Nudity was probably the norm, at least in the south of Europe.

p. 68 *Sonnet 6*. The attempt to relate fashion to political, economic and social change is often made, but it remains a bit of a mystery. Does a higher hem-line really presage a new openness and reluctance to follow traditional leadership? Götterdämmerung means the twilight of the gods (Wagner's *Ring* cycle ends with an opera called that) and therefore the end of the world, like an Apocalypse.

p. 69 Sonnet 7. A reflection on the artist's life. The 'oldest profession' usually means the prostitute's. Like her, we have no real claim on the city, we offer for cash the beauties of nakedness to passers-by we don't know.

p.70 Sonnet 8. The Field of the Cloth of Gold was an enormous example of conspicuous consumption by the feudal nobility of England and France, as the young Henry VIII met Francis I to discuss peace. The result was that the English Treasury almost bankrupted itself. 'The field full of folk' was Langland's phrase for the whole people of England in his long poem *Piers Plowman*. So, who as artists are we to serve? The boss class or the people as a whole?

Cotton was an expensive fabric as long as the fibre had to be pulled out of the bolls (or seedheads) by hand. The cotton gin (invented by a New Englander) did it mechanically and made it possible for cotton to be the first industrially mass-produced fabric. This created a huge labour shortage to work the cotton plantations in the Southern States. The use of black slaves to fill the gap led to the American Civil War; and because the raw cotton was then taken to Lancashire, which had both the climate and the engineering know-how to spin and weave it on a massive scale, it became the main source of Britain's industrial might and the driving force behind British imperialism. For the first time, poor people all over the world could afford new clothes. The power to make and sell cheap cloth was almost a British monopoly until at least the last quarter of the nineteenth century.

p. 71 *Sonnet 9*. Gandhi's effort to make Indians produce their own cloth in the villages was probably misguided in the long term, but it did threaten the way they took British monopolies for granted and so prepared them for independence.

p.72 *Sonnet 10*. Dulas Ward. Based on my last experience in hospital. The nurses' cotton or cotton-substitute uniforms define an order and establish their obvious humanity as against the chaotically disfunctional patients. Zimmers are walking frames. Exo-skeletons, like a crab's or insect's, have the hard bits outside the soft, not inside like bones.

p.73 *Sonnet 11*. Remembers a Christian holocaust – there've been quite a lot, as in the Sudan today. Returns to fabrics as religious or memorial confrontations with the dead. A white chasuble (sacred poncho) is worn by the priest at Christmastide masses.

p.74 *Sonnet 12*. Costume-making/designing is one of the oldest sacred arts, like singing, drumming and dancing – and poetry – as part of shamanistic ritual. There are pictures in the cave-paintings of men dressed as deer or antelopes, wearing animal masks. As artists, we still perform something of this function, though its sacredness is only vestigially felt. We both create new feeling-patterns for the living to walk in, and reassure the dead that we still belong. They can safely give ground to the new imaginative world that the living need.

p.75 *Sonnet 13*. 'Retting' is the technical term for rotting the soft tissues of the flax so that the fibres can be easily extracted. Linen, like all cellulose fabrics, is quite hard to colour with natural dyes. Wool and silk are protein-based and generally much easier. Osiris was a vegetation god who ritually died and rose again every year. Popular mystery-religions were founded on his cult, which, like Christianity, offered immortality to all, not just to the Pharaohs, the god-kings. Ra is the chief god of the Egyptians, the sun-god and divine father of the Pharaohs.

p.76 *Sonnet 14*. Penelope is using an upright, primitive loom where the warps hang weighted from a beam and the shuttle is pushed through by hand after the required warps have been shedded with a stick, again by hand. She is not weaving any old cloth of course, but tapestry (not like Bayeux, an embroidery) which is anyway a slow business and hard to mechanise. She is in fact weaving the equivalent of an epic poem, to give fame and glory to her husband Odysseus. The Odyssey tells how she was pestered by suitors when Odysseus did not return after the Trojan War. She deferred making a decision until she'd finished her tapestry, but every night she secretly undid the work she'd done on it the day before. I've made this an act of artistic dissatisfaction, not a mere trick to fool the suitors.

p.77 *Sonnet 15*. Eleusis was the site of a Greek mystery religion (see note to 13.) Candidates had to endure various trials – solitude, fear, tests leading to a ritual 'death' – before they were initiated and returned in triumph to their city where they were welcomed as heroes reborn.

p.78 *Sonnet 16*. Silk is unwound from the discarded chrysalids of a moth that lives only on one kind of mulberry tree in China. See also the nursery rhyme, 'Here we go round the mulberry bush.' Finally, as artists, we become like silkworms. shrouding with white seed (the chrysalids) tomorrow's ground.

Symphony 9: Everworlds

p.91 *Second Movement*

Robert Graves

Robert Graves, half-Irish, half-German, went to public school near Oxford but spent the holidays at his parents' house in Harlech. On the outbreak of war in 1914, he joined the Royal Welsh Fusiliers. He was wounded, reported dead, and disabled by war neurosis. He married and went up to Oxford as a student. Laura Riding, the American poet, arrived in England in 1926. She and Graves had a tumultuous and crisis-ridden relationship, which included her attempted suicide and the break-up of his marriage. He treated her as a poetic master and submitted all his work to her for approval or criticism. She deserted both Graves and poetry in 1939, returning to America to live with Schyler Jackson. The impetus to write *The White Goddess,* a 'grammar of poetic myth', seems to have come from his need to defend poetry (as well as himself) against her rejection.

Graves had lived in Dejà, Mallorca, with Laura Riding before the 1939-45 war, and returned there afterwards with Beryl, who became his second wife. He died and is buried there.

The tulip-tree in the last verse is actually not in his garden in Mallorca but an unconscious memory of a poem he wrote in America, 'The Moon ends in Nightmare', when he realized that Laura had changed and her behaviour had become monstrous. But even when I realised this, the tulip-tree would not let go, even if I'd known how to change it. It seemed to have a talisman-value for Graves himself that I was loath to meddle with.